❋ Hannah Lyons Johnson ❋

Let's Make Jam

photographs by Daniel Dorn, Jr.

Lothrop, Lee & Shepard Company ❋ New York

Books by Hannah Lyons Johnson

Let's Make Jam
Photographs by Daniel Dorn, Jr.

From Seed to Jack-o'-Lantern
Photographs by Daniel Dorn, Jr.

Let's Bake Bread
Photographs by Daniel Dorn, Jr.

Hello, Small Sparrow
Illustrated by Tony Chen

Text copyright © 1975 by Hannah Lyons Johnson
Photographs copyright © 1975 by Daniel Dorn, Jr.

All rights reserved. No part of this book may be reproduced or utilized in any form or by any means, electronic or mechanical, including photocopying, recording or by any information retrieval system, without permission in writing from the Publisher. Inquiries should be addressed to Lothrop, Lee and Shepard Company, 105 Madison Ave., New York, N.Y. 10016.
Printed in the United States of America.
1 2 3 4 5 79 78 77 76 75

Library of Congress Cataloging in Publication Data

Johnson, Hannah Lyons.
  Let's make jam.

    SUMMARY: Step-by-step process of making jam, from picking the fruit until the jam is bottled.
  1. Jam—Juvenile literature. [1. Jam 2. Cookery] I. Dorn, Daniel, ill. II. Title.
TX612.J3J64   641.8'52   74-20806
ISBN 0-688-41682-9
ISBN 0-688-51682-3 (lib. bdg.)

✻ Let's Make Jam ✻

Special thanks to our berry-picking jam makers, Tracy and Matthew Walter and Dylan Johnson

✻ Introduction ✻

Strawberries are one of spring's special delights. They nestle in their patches, peeking out from under leaf green canopies, plump and red and tempting, just waiting to be picked and tasted. They are beautiful to look at, heavenly to smell and delicious to eat. People enjoy stitching them in needlework, photographing and painting them; but most of all people enjoy eating them.

Strawberry plants are bought at a nursery and are planted in rows in the fields in early spring. They are not allowed to produce fruit the first year they are planted so that they will be stronger plants and bear more fruit the following spring. Pinching off the flowers and buds prevents the berries from forming this first year.

As each plant develops it sends out runners that become new strawberry plants. In the fall the plants are covered with straw or hay (this is called mulch) to keep them from freezing or being damaged by cold weather. When the plants begin to grow again the following spring, the mulch is raked away from the plants into the middle of the rows. It is put back on the plants if there is a frost, to prevent the flowers and buds from being killed.

Strawberries form in the centers of the female flowers after they have been fertilized with pollen grains from the male flowers. Pollen grains are tiny yellow granules in the centers of the male flowers which are usually transferred

to the female flowers by bees. After the tiny berries have been fertilized, the petals dry up and fall off the flowers and the green berries grow into full size strawberries that gradually turn red and ripe and are ready for the pickers.

The growing season for strawberries is sadly short. We just get used to having them around and poof—they disappear from the fields, markets and farm stands. There is one way to keep strawberries around all year, though, and that is by making them into jam. On a raw winter's morning you can spread homemade strawberry jam on your hot toast and be reminded of warm spring days.

The recipe in this book makes an old-fashioned, longer-cooking type of jam. It's the kind your grandmothers and great-grandmothers used to make. The jam has no artificial ingredients or preservatives in it. It will take you about $1\frac{1}{2}$ hours to make or put up your jam. It would be a good idea to read the whole book through once before you start so you will know exactly what you will be doing.

❋ How Does Jam Happen? ❋

Four things are necessary to produce jam.

1. *Fruit:* Fruit gives jam its flavor. Jam can be made from any fresh or frozen fruit.

2. *Pectin:* Pectin is a natural chemical substance found in all fruits. It helps the jam to thicken or gel. Some fruits have more pectin than others. Apples are high in pectin while strawberries are low. Also, underripe fruit has more pectin than fully ripe fruit.

3. *Acid:* Acid is another chemical substance found in all fruits. It helps the jam to gel and also adds to its flavor.

4. *Sugar:* Sugar has a big part in jam making. It has been used for centuries as a preservative, which means it helps to keep food from spoiling. Sugar preserves the jam, adds to its flavor, and also helps it to gel. And the fruit is kept firm by the sugar.

✺ Some Things You Will Need ✺

1. 4 or 5 ½-pint canning jars with lids and screw-on caps (they can be bought at hardware stores or in houseware sections of department stores).
2. colander
3. potato masher
4. large bowl
5. large stainless steel or enamel flat-bottomed pot with high sides. Aluminum, iron, or copper pots might discolor the fruit.
6. pot big enough to hold the jars, lids, and caps
7. slotted spoon
8. small paring knife
9. large measuring cup
10. potholders
11. damp, clean sponge
12. tongs
13. ladle
14. long-handled wooden spoon
15. clean dish towel
16. baking pan
17. timer, if you have one

Jam is extremely hot when it is cooking. For this reason as well as the fact that you will be working with a hot stove and hot jars, you should have an adult with you who can supervise your safety and do some of the hotter jobs for you.

❋ What Goes Into Jam? ❋

1. 2 heaping quarts of fresh strawberries. About $\frac{1}{4}$ of them should be barely ripe because they contain more pectin than fully ripe berries. Or you can use enough whole frozen berries (2-4 packages, depending on the size of the berries) to equal 2 quarts of fresh berries. Be sure to defrost the berries before you start to make the jam.
2. 3 cups of sugar.
3. $\frac{1}{2}$ lemon.

❄ Step 1/Wash-up ❄

After you have gathered all the ingredients and utensils together, wash your hands and fingernails very well and you will be ready to begin.

Start by washing the jars, lids, and caps in warm soapy water and rinsing them well in hot water.

Put the washed jars, lids, and caps in a large pot and cover them with hot water. The jars should be right side up and filled with water too. Place the pot on the stove, cover it, and bring the water to a boil. Turn off the heat and set the pot aside till a little later. Boiling the water kills any bacteria on the jars, lids, or caps that might spoil your jam.

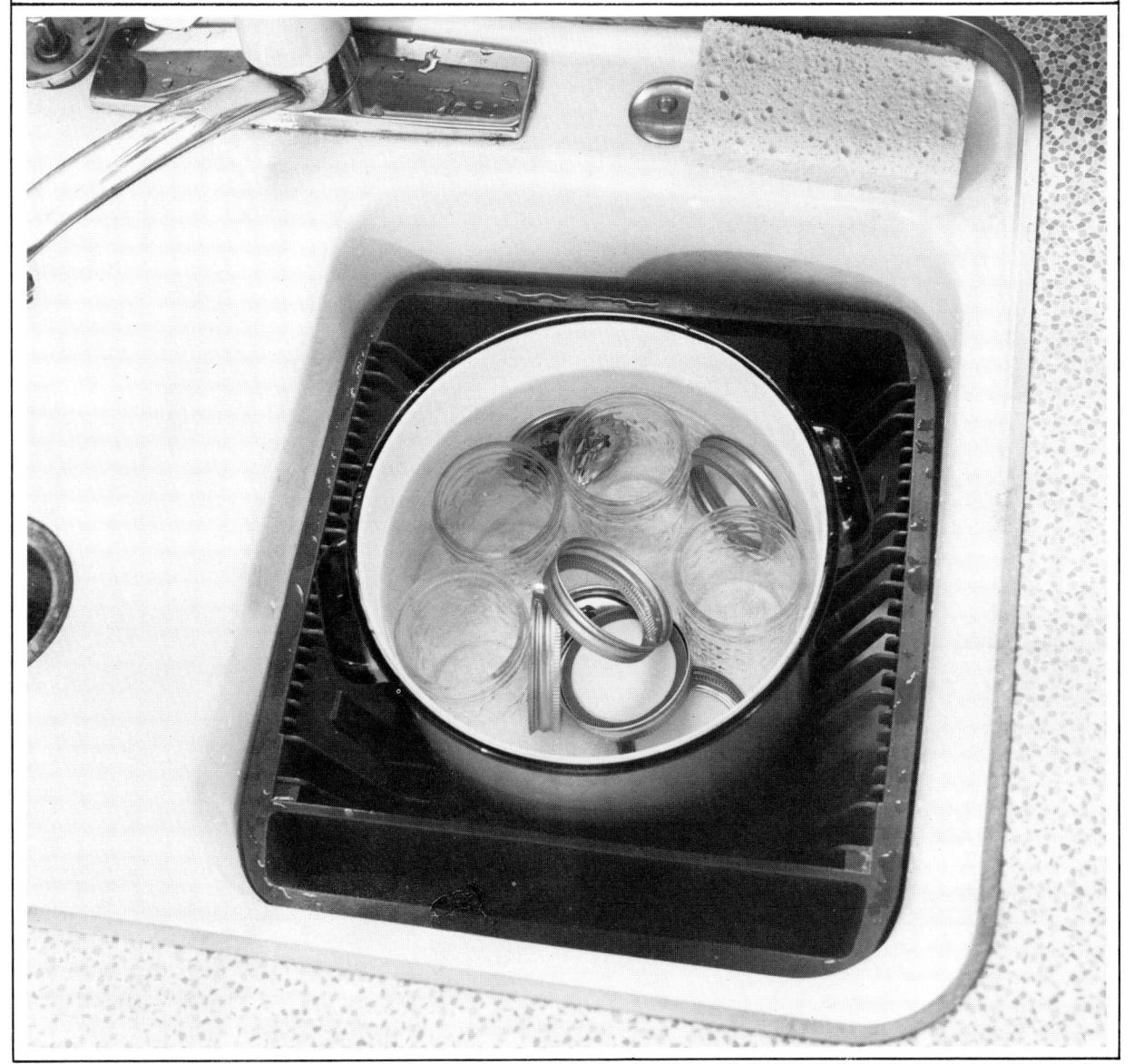

❋ Step 2/The Sugar ❋

With the help of an adult, set the oven at 150° (very low). Pour the 3 cups of sugar into a baking pan and spread it out evenly on the bottom with a spoon. Put the pan of sugar in the oven to warm while you're preparing the berries. (The warm sugar will dissolve faster. This cuts down on the cooking time as well as lessening the chance of having crunchy sugar crystals in your finished jam.)

❋ Step 3/Preparing the Berries ❋

Put the berries into the colander and wash them under cold running water.

With a small (not too sharp) paring knife, carefully cut the green tops off the berries. Also cut out and throw away any brown or rotted spots in the berries. If the berries are large, cut them into eighths. If they are medium size, cut them into quarters, and if small into halves.

Put the cut berries into a large mixing bowl and mash them down with the potato masher. This releases the juice in the berries to provide enough moisture for cooking and makes them small enough so you won't have big lumps in your jam.

(If you like jam with bigger chunks of fruit, don't mash the berries too much.)

Pour the mashed berries into the cooking pot and set them aside.

❊ Step 4/The Combination ❊

Take the pan of warm sugar from the oven, being sure to use a potholder. (The pan will be hot enough to burn you.)

Stir through the sugar with a spoon to break up the crustiness on top. The sugar will pour from the pan more easily this way.

Pour the sugar into the pot containing the crushed berries and stir the sugar and berries together very well.

❋ Step 5/Cooking ❋

Remember to be safety-conscious when you cook. Be sure to stand back from the stove, because the boiling mixture will splatter some. Loose-fitting clothes aren't good to wear when you are cooking, because they can brush against the burner and catch fire or dip into the pot.

Put the pot on the stove and turn the burner on to medium high heat. Keep stirring the mixture quickly with the wooden spoon for several minutes until it really starts to boil hard. (A hard boil can't be stirred down with your

spoon.) This is the moment when you set the timer for exactly 20 minutes. (If you don't have a timer, keep track of the time by checking your kitchen clock.)

As the berry and sugar mixture boils, it will foam up in the pot a bit and be very steamy.

Drag the wooden spoon slowly along the bottom of the pot to keep the mixture from sticking to the bottom and burning. (You use a wooden spoon because it won't get hot in your hand.)

The mixture will gradually start to thicken as it boils.

After the mixture has cooked for about 15 minutes, have an adult remove the jars, lids and tops from the hot water with the tongs and set them on the dish towel to dry.

Be sure the jars are not in a draft. They must be hot when you are ready to fill them so the hot jam won't crack them.

When the timer rings (or when 20 minutes are up), turn off the burner.

There will be a thick pink foam on the jam. Skim it off with the slotted spoon and put it in a dish to be thrown away when it's cool.

Squeeze several drops of juice from $1/2$ lemon over the jam and stir this juice in well (be careful not to drop any lemon pits into the jam). The lemon juice adds more acid and cuts down on the sweetness of the sugar.

❋ Step 6/Filling & Sealing the Jars ❋

Fill and seal one jar at a time. Sealing the jars keeps out bacteria which might spoil the jam and keeps in all the freshness and flavor.

Using the ladle, fill a jar with the hot jam to $\frac{1}{8}$ inch from the top. Wipe off any spills from the rim of the jar with the damp, clean sponge.

Place the lid on top of the jar with the rubber ring touching the glass.

Screw the cap on tightly.

Wipe the outside of the jar thoroughly to remove any drips or spills which might attract ants to the storage shelf.

This recipe will make 4 ½ pint jars of jam with perhaps a little bit left over. You can put this in a small clean jar in the refrigerator for your morning toast! The amount of jam you get will depend on the amount of juice in the fruit and the length of time you cook it. Jam cooked for 20 minutes is fairly thick. If you want it to be thicker cook it 1–5 minutes more. If you want it thinner cook it 1–5 minutes less. Remember, though, that jam thickens a little more as it cools.

❊ Step 7/Storing Your Homemade Jam ❊

Let the jars stand on your counter or table until they have cooled. Then tighten the caps again and label the jars with the name of the jam and the date you made it.

Store the jars on a nice cool, dark shelf somewhere in your home. (Light will cause the jam to darken and lose its wonderful bright color. Heat will destroy the fresh flavor.)

Jam will keep this way for many, many months, but your family will probably eat it all up before many, many months can pass!

❋ Step 8/Clean-up ❋

The last thing to do is wash all the utensils you have used and put them away. Leaving the kitchen as clean and orderly as you found it will certainly be appreciated.

❋ Some Afterwords & Alternatives ❋

Once you make this jam you will probably want to try other recipes. There are lots of cookbooks containing jam recipes in your local library, and if you are really lucky you will have a jam-making relative who will share some old family recipe secrets with you. There are many different ways of making jam.

Some people like to use commercial pectin in their jams. This pectin is available at your market and comes in both powdered and liquid form and it contains chemicals and artificial ingredients. If you want to try some, be sure to follow the directions on the package or bottle. You won't have to cook the jam as long, but you will have to use more sugar.

Many people don't buy special canning jars but instead use jars they have saved from other foods, like peanut butter or pickles. If you want to use saved jars, wash, rinse and boil them just as this recipe states. With these jars, the sealing is done with hot melted wax called paraffin. This can be a very dangerous process and should be done only by an adult. The complete directions for using paraffin are on the paraffin package. Paraffin sometimes cracks and isn't suitable if you are planning to send your jam through the mail. The rough handling that packages get would probably break or loosen the paraffin seal and the jam would leak out.

Last of all, don't try to make a bigger batch of jam by doubling the recipe. You would have to cook the jam longer which would destroy some of the fresh flavor and color.

❄ A Gift of Spring ❄

The jam you make can be used with many things. Aside from being perfect with peanut butter, it makes a terrific topping for ice cream and pudding or a good filling for cookies. Perhaps the best thing you can do with your homemade jam is give it away to someone you love. A jar of jam* makes a very special gift which may remind that someone of spring—the yearly miracle.

*You might want to ask that the jars be returned to you when they are empty to be refilled from your next batch of jam!

About the Author

Hannah Lyons Johnson is the author of Lothrop's highly popular *From Seed to Jack-o'-Lantern, Let's Bake Bread,* and *Hello, Small Sparrow.* She is a former elementary school teacher whose interests include baking, handicrafts, and literature. Ms. Johnson lives in New Jersey with her husband and two young sons.

About the Photographer

Daniel Dorn, Jr. is a self-employed professional photographer who especially enjoys photographing children. He also took the pictures for Ms. Johnson's *Let's Bake Bread* and *From Seed to Jack-o'-Lantern.* Mr. Dorn lives in New Jersey with his wife and two young daughters.